COMMON SENSE LEADERSHIP

COMMON SENSE LEADERSHIP

A HANDBOOK FOR SUCCESS AS A LEADER

by ROGER FULTON

TEN SPEED PRESS
BERKELEY, CALIFORNIA

1🖐️

TEN SPEED PRESS
P.O. Box 7123
Berkeley, CA 94707

Cover design by Toni Tajima
Typesetting by Jeff Brandenburg, ImageComp

Library of Congress Cataloging-in-Publication Data

Fulton, Roger.
    Common sense leadership : a handbook for success as
a leader / by Roger Fulton.
          p.   cm.
    ISBN 0-89815-743-9
    1. Leadership. I. Title.
    BF637.L4F85   1995
    303.3'4—dc20   95-144
                                                          CIP

Printed in Canada
FIRST PRINTING 1995

        3   4   5   —   99   98   97

TABLE OF CONTENTS

INTRODUCTION vii

CHAPTER ONE
A Leader Prepares 1

CHAPTER TWO
A Leader Is 17

CHAPTER THREE
A Leader Supervises By 39

CHAPTER FOUR
A Leader Manages By 55

CHAPTER FIVE
A Leader Understands 71

CHAPTER SIX
A Leader Leads By 89

CHAPTER SEVEN
A Leader Avoids 103

CONCLUSION 129

APPENDIX I 131
Twenty-five negative behavioral characteristics
that can hinder potential leaders

APPENDIX II 132
Twenty-five positive behavioral characteristics
that can help potential leaders

INTRODUCTION: CAN ANYONE LEAD?

*N*OT *JUST* ANYONE. However, anyone who has the desire to lead, who is willing to make the commitment to being a leader and who prepares themselves properly, can become a leader.

Leadership requires the knowledge necessary to understand the leadership role, the training to perform the day-to-day activities required of a leader, and a sound foundation of experience upon which to base future decisions.

This preparation is absolutely necessary, but the most important quality necessary to be a leader is desire. The desire to lead the way. The desire to take on difficult problems. The desire to go a step beyond. And, of course, the desire to be a leader of others.

> *Anyone can hold the helm when the sea is calm.*
> Publilius Syrus

WHY BE A LEADER?

Leadership is the art of influencing and directing people in such a way as to obtain their willing obedience, confidence, respect and cooperation.

Anyone can be boss, but the person who has personnel working with, rather than for or under, him or her is the *true* leader of people.

Your leadership responsibilities will include:

1. Accomplishment of organizational objectives
2. Welfare of the organization's personnel

You must satisfy both subordinates, peers and superiors. Keep in mind that you can't lead by yourself: you need someone to follow you!

You don't have to be a genius to be a leader. Most leaders are people of slightly above-average intelligence.

Leadership is not a mysterious phenomenon. It is a combination of skills and observable behaviors that can be learned. This book can help you to learn those skills and behaviors.

WHAT DO LEADERS DO?

There is an enormous difference between those who want to squirt oil on the machinery and those who want to build new machinery.

Strong leadership can help design and build the new machinery with innovative features and outstanding workmanship.

Leaders get people excited!

They build on strengths, rather than dwelling on weaknesses.

People willingly sign up to serve under outstanding leaders.

Truly effective leaders combine supervisory, managerial and leadership skills to get the best from their people and themselves.

Supervisors, managers and leaders share some of the same tasks, but it is the way they perform them, the way they treat the people involved, that distinguishes leaders from the rest of the pack.

As an example, supervisors supervise and managers control, but leaders create commitment and are absolutely essential in times of chaos, crisis or change.

While supervisors and managers cover the more technical aspects of business, such as getting the basic tasks done, leaders are people with inspiration and vision.

Leaders take pride in their accomplishments. When things are running routinely, a manger can maintain the status quo. But when there is a crisis, somebody has to take charge. That's the leader!

CAN YOU BE A LEADER?

Leadership **can** be learned! Reading the following pages can get you started down the most exciting road you will ever travel.

Good Luck!!!

> *I'm a great believer in luck; and I find the harder I work, the more I have of it.*
>
> Stephen Leacock

❧ CHAPTER ONE: A LEADER PREPARES

*P*REPARING YOURSELF to be a leader can be as critical to future success as any subsequent actions you may take. There are several tips in this chapter on how to get yourself started. Read them carefully.

If you don't believe that adequate preparation is necessary, just read what our panel of experts has to say:

> *The man who is prepared has his battle half-fought.*
> Cervantes

> *I will prepare and some day my chance will come.*
> Abraham Lincoln

> *Before everything else, getting ready is the secret of success.*
> Henry Ford

MASTERING THE BASICS

A leader must possess many qualities and master many skills. Which leadership qualities and skills do you already possess? Which do you lack? Which can you cultivate?

If you haven't already done so, we suggest that you read *Common Sense Supervision: A Handbook For Success As a Supervisor*, also by Roger Fulton.

It will give you great insight into the basics of supervision and management, and will give you a sound foundation for successful leadership.

The book is also available from Ten Speed Press, P.O. Box 7123, Berkeley, CA 94707. For information on how to order, call 1-800-841-BOOK.

The question, "Who ought to be boss?" is like asking "Who ought to be tenor in the quartet?" Obviously the man who can sing tenor.

Henry Ford

LEARNING FROM THE PAST

Leadership is not new!

Leadership successes and failures have been going on since man discovered fire (and occasionally got burned).

In this book, we take advantage of the wisdom of the ages whenever possible. The words of wisdom from dozens of successful leaders throughout the centuries will help us to comprehend and remember the skills necessary for our own leadership successes.

The farther back you can look, the farther forward you are likely to see.

Winston Churchill

GAINING KNOWLEDGE

Knowledge of your industry, and the various components which make up that industry, is absolutely necessary for success.

You must have a high degree of technical competence to be successful.

You must study your industry from an intellectual, as well as a practical, perspective to get the big picture of your industry and its relationship with the rest of the world.

Leaders read trade magazines, newsletters and related publications. They belong to professional organizations and attend professional trade shows, educational seminars and appropriate social functions.

Leaders strive to be the most knowledgeable and professional people in their field.

> *The essence of knowledge is, living it, to apply it; not having it, to confess your ignorance.*
>
> Confucius

DEVELOPING A VARIED BACKGROUND

Leaders develop a broad-based background of knowledge and experience they can draw from when necessary.

They develop this background by actively participating in sports, social organizations, church activities, and charity work.

Leaders interact with other people.

They participate in business discussions and activities, and gain knowledge and experience in design, production, marketing, sales and delivery systems.

> *Since we cannot be universal and know all that is to be known of everything, we ought to know a little about everything.*
>
> Blaise Pascal

GAINING EXPERIENCE

Prospective leaders gain practical experience in their own or related fields.

They make an extra effort to gain more experience than their peers by *getting involved.*

They can draw on diverse experiences from a variety of sources as they prepare for the future.

> *However thou are read in the theory, if thou has not practice, thou are ignorant.*
>
> Sadi

STAYING UP-TO-DATE

Leaders know about and utilize the latest in new technology and procedures.

Leaders are aware of trends within their own industry, the nation, and the world.

By belonging to professional associations and reading journals, newsletters and other publications, leaders can prepare to be on the leading edge of new technology.

The closer you are to the future, the easier it is to predict.

> *Destiny is not a matter of chance; it is a matter of choice. It is not something to be waited for; but rather something to be achieved.*
>
> William Jennings Bryan

SHARING INTERNAL INFORMATION

Within your own organization, there are other people and departments that have knowledge and resources you can draw on to enhance your own unit's performance.

Prepare for the future by initiating and cultivating personal relationships with your counterparts in other areas so you can share resources and information with them.

Some of the other departments with which you may want to share information may include marketing, sales, manufacturing, customer service, personnel, and finance.

> *Coming together is a beginning; keeping together is progress; working together is success.*
>
> Henry Ford

OBTAINING OUTSIDE INFORMATION

Relying solely on internal information is not enough for a leader to develop the vision needed to lead the way.

Leaders are the key to bringing outside information into an organization. They meet with other executives, participate in trade shows and meetings, meet and talk with customers, suppliers, and people in related industries to find out what is—or should be—new in their industry and what they can learn from other industries.

They recognize that they must improve faster and better than their competitors to remain the best.

Knowledge and human power are synonymous.
Francis Baron

BECOMING A GOOD PUBLIC SPEAKER

Some people come by this skill naturally, but not many. Most have to learn it.

It is not hard. Most adult education programs and colleges have a course for beginners.

When you must speak in public, always:

Be prepared.

Know your audience.

Speak from prepared notes (in case you lose your place).

Be positive and confident in your presentation.

> *Speech is power: speech is to persuade, to convert, to compel.*
>
> Ralph Waldo Emerson

CONDUCTING RESEARCH

Doing Your Homework. Nothing replaces detailed research on a specific topic.

Leaders utilize a variety of sources of information to avoid problems and develop a successful project.

In addition to routine trade journals, newsletters and magazines, leaders actually go to the library to research critical topics.

Knowledge is power, and leaders know how to develop that power better than their peers.

The next best thing to knowing something is knowing where to find it.

Samuel Johnson

GAINING RESPECT

Gaining the respect of peers, subordinates and those above you in the organization should be a major goal of yours as an aspiring leader. Gaining the respect of your competitors and those in related industries should also be a major goal.

Your reputation for competence and fairness is so valuable that you must always consider it as a factor in all aspects of your work.

If you can be liked and respected at the same time, you are a *true* leader. If you can only achieve one, be sure you are respected.

Respect yourself if you would have others respect you.
Baltasar Gracián

WINNING LOYALTY

Leaders must be able to garner the support of their subordinates and bosses in order to be successful.

Loyalty must be earned. It is earned by caring about and protecting both subordinates and bosses. It is earned by working *with* people and helping *them* be successful.

The loyalty and dedication of subordinates can help leaders to meet difficult deadlines or solve difficult problems. The loyalty of a boss can get leaders out of potential trouble or help minimize errors.

Over time, leaders who have proven that they are worthy of subordinates' and bosses' support will have great loyalty from all.

Loyalty is the one thing a leader cannot do without.
A. P. Goethey

DEVELOPING CONFIDENCE

Subordinates must have confidence in their leader. They must have the confidence to believe that their leader knows what he/she is doing.

They must believe that the leader has the vision and ability to get the job done.

Such confidence comes from previous successes.

Over time, subordinates, and superiors as well, will have faith and confidence in a successful leader.

In quietness and in confidence shall be your strength.
Isaiah 30:15

DEVELOPING A SENSE OF HUMOR

Humor is important to help keep things in perspective, for both leaders and their subordinates.

A sense of humor can ease tensions during difficult times and a little humor can help brighten anyone's day.

> *If I had no sense of humor, I would long ago have committed suicide.*
>
> Mahatma Gandhi

*T*HERE ARE MANY ATTRIBUTES that leaders possess. Virtually all of them can be learned.

The following pages list attributes you should work on if being a leader is your goal.

> *In the great mass of our people there are plenty of individuals of intelligence from among whom leadership can be recruited.*
>
> Herbert Hoover

COURAGEOUS

Both physically and morally, leaders must have the personal courage to try something new:
  To go where others fear to tread,
  To face adversity, and to support their people.
  To protect their subordinates from unfairness.
  To stand up to their superiors whenever necessary.

> *It is courage, courage, courage that raises the blood of life to crimson splendor.*
>
> George Bernard Shaw

DEPENDABLE

Leaders are as dependable as the day is long.
   Leaders keep promises, are always on time, and can be relied upon to fulfill any duty or obligation.

> *A little neglect may breed great mischief . . . for the want of a shoe the horse was lost; and for the want of a horse the rider was lost.*
>
> Benjamin Franklin

TACTFUL

Leaders think before they speak.

Tact should be used with subordinates, bosses, customers and suppliers.

Being tactful costs nothing, but may be rewarded many times over in good will and solid relationships.

Tact: the ability to describe others as they see themselves.
Abraham Lincoln

UNSELFISH

Leaders always share, or give away, credit for successes.

Leaders give of their time to others to make their jobs and lives easier.

In everything they do, they exhibit the attitude of sharing, except when things go wrong. Then, the *true* leader accepts the blame and shares it with no one.

> *He who wishes to secure the good of others, has already secured his own.*
>
> Confucius

HUMBLE

Leaders live for success, yet they should be humble when the accolades start to flow.

True leaders say "thank you" for compliments and point to their subordinates and say "They did it."

Leaders have egos, but they keep them under control.

> *A hundred times a day I remind myself that my life depends on the labors of other men, living and dead, and that I must exert myself in order to give, in the measure as I have received, and am still receiving.*
>
> Albert Einstein

OPTIMISTIC

Leaders view each day as full of challenges which are a pleasure to meet and conquer.

Leaders always view a cup as being half full, not half empty.

They know that planning and organization, coupled with good personnel, properly directed by a *true* leader, will always lead to success.

Repeatedly making all the right moves makes optimism come naturally.

A leader is a dealer in hope.
Napoleon I

CREATIVE

Leaders develop new and innovative solutions to problems.

No problem is too great.

No solution is impossible to find.

Thinking creatively is the leader's stock in trade.

In thinking creatively, a *true* leader dares to be bold.

There is one thing stronger than all the armies in the world, and that is an idea whose time has come.

Victor Hugo

CONFIDENT

True leaders can maintain a calm, internal confidence because they have worked hard, prepared for the tough moments, and have built on the successes of the past.

In fact, leaders *must* appear confident at all times, especially when the pressure is on.

A professional bearing and demeanor are outward signs of self-assurance and an ability to handle the situation at hand.

The confidence possessed by a *true* leader is perceived by others and they too will believe in you and your ability to handle the situation.

True leaders feel good about themselves and their ability. And it shows.

> *Calm self-confidence is as far from conceit, as the desire to earn a decent living is remote from greed.*
> Channing Pollock

ENERGETIC

Leaders target the task at hand, then focus all of their energies toward the successful attainment of that goal.

When the task is complete, leaders rest their energy momentarily, until the next task appears.

Leaders must have strong personal energy to get a project up and running. They must also maintain that energy to see projects through to completion.

Energy and persistence conquer all things.
Benjamin Franklin

INTELLIGENT

Leaders have above-average intelligence, but not necessarily much above average.

Leaders must have the ability to analyze, evaluate and comprehend. To do so requires basic intelligence, coupled with hard work, dedication and commitment to the task at hand.

Once committed, leaders can overshadow people with greater intelligence because they use their resources to the fullest.

> *The man who acquires the ability to take full possession of his own mind, may take possession of anything else to which he is justly entitled.*
>
> Andrew Carnegie

HONEST

Scrupulously honest!

They never consider kickbacks, cheating or fraud. Their integrity is unquestioned.

Their peers, subordinates, bosses and competitors know it, and respect and trust them as a result.

> *No public man can be just a little crooked.*
> Herbert Hoover

CONSISTENT

No hot and cold here!
    Their subordinates always know what to expect.
    Their peers always know what to expect.
    Their bosses always know what to expect.
    In leadership, the best surprise is no surprise, for subordinates, peers, and bosses alike.

> *We are what we repeatedly do.*
> Aristotle

LOYAL

Leaders are loyal:
    To their subordinates.
    To their organization.
    To their bosses.
    We're not talking about *blind* loyalty.
    Occasionally, loyalty even means constructive disagreement with a boss or a subordinate, for the good of all.

> *An ounce of loyalty is worth a pound of cleverness.*
> Elbert Hubbard

MATURE

No kids' games!

When the lives and livelihoods of others are at stake, there is no room for rash actions or petty bickering.

Leaders, whatever their age, must be mature enough to face challenges and handle consequences in a cool and professional manner.

Emotional maturity is exhibited by leaders who are neither crushed by defeat nor overly elated by victory.

Think like a man of action, act like a man of thought.
Henri-Louis Bergson

SINCERE

No false pretenses here!

If a leader tells a subordinate that they did a good job, then it must have been good.

Insincerity destroys the credibility of leaders and renders them ineffective.

Always be sincere and warm.

Sincerity is the highest compliment you can pay.
Ralph Waldo Emerson

ADAPTIVE

Change is welcomed by a *true* leader, even in mid-stream.

Human beings can adjust to almost anything, if they want to. Leaders ensure that others see the need to adjust or change, and they help them through the transition.

Leaders build a degree of flexibility into their plans to allow for unexpected changes. Leaders are willing to make changes when they are warranted.

The unexpected always happens.
Lawrence J. Peters

TENACIOUS

Leaders don't let go!

They keep striving toward success until it is obtained.

If their idea didn't fly this year, it will be presented again next year, and it will be even better.

Ultimately, their tenacity will endure and their vision will be realized.

> *There is no failure except in no longer trying.*
> Kin Hubbard

PERSONABLE

Leaders are friendly, not arrogant or egotistical.

They are as friendly with the janitors as they are with the chairman of the board.

Leaders are open enough so that everyone around them can get to know and trust them.

Leaders are also approachable. Anyone can talk to *true* leaders and present a problem or idea to them without ridicule or repercussions.

True leaders are recognized as warm and likable people.

> *You can make more friends in two months by becoming interested in other people than you can in two years by trying to get other people interested in you.*
>
> Dale Carnegie

FAIR

Leaders are fair to everyone:
  Subordinates.
  Customers.
  Co-workers.
  The organization.
  And to themselves.

> *To thine own self be true; And it followeth as the night*
> *the day, thou cans't then be false to any man.*
> William Shakespeare

PATIENT

Patience has long been lauded as a great virtue.
It remains so in today's hectic world.
Leaders who exhibit patience with all whom they encounter will gain lasting respect.

He that can have patience, can have what he will.
Benjamin Franklin

WHAT DO LEADERS actually do when supervising their people? Their subordinates know the answer.

After all, who sees leaders more clearly than the subordinates?

Would your subordinates elect you to your present position?

> *We confide in our strength, without boasting of it; we respect that of others, without fearing it.*
>
> Thomas Jefferson

BEING A GOOD FOLLOWER

Leaders do what they are told, willingly and to the best of their ability.

They pursue the goals and objectives of the organization.

We are all subordinate to someone. Leaders must be sure they fully understand that.

> *The high destiny of the individual is to serve rather than to rule.*
>
> Albert Einstein

RECOGNIZING GOOD WORK

Leaders recognize good work as quickly as they recognize poor work.

It is important for leaders to provide positive reinforcement and constructive feedback to subordinates.

Leaders also recognize the contribution that every member of the team makes to the success of the organization.

People want approval from the boss as well as from their peers. *True* leaders give it to them.

> *The deepest principle of human nature is the craving to be appreciated.*
>
> William James

CREATING COMMITMENT

This is not an easy task!

Leaders get others to *join the team*, to *get on board*, and work toward a common goal. Under that leadership, subordinates join up because they *want* to.

Leaders use small successes to build up employees' confidence and motivate them to do more. People naturally respond to such a challenge.

Leaders encourage their people to do better, to push themselves a little harder, not for money, but for the recognition of a job well done. Leaders instill personal pride in their people.

A leader's enthusiasm for his own work carries over to the other members of the team, who soon have the same enthusiasm for *their* work.

Subordinates should ultimately look at a project and say, "This is ours," and "I contributed."

> *To maintain a joyful family requires much from both the parents and the children. Each member of the family has to become, in a special way, the servant of the others.*
> Pope John Paul II

ENCOURAGING COOPERATION

Leaders encourage cooperation between subordinates, bosses and various departments of the organization.

In general, they all are seeking the same final goal. However, that long-range, final goal is often clouded in territorialism, petty bickering, jealousies and ego gratification.

True leaders can make a real difference by ensuring that they do all they can to encourage everyone to work together for the common good.

> *Light is the task, where many share the task.*
> Homer

EXPECTING HIGH QUALITY AND QUANTITY

Leaders get the high quality and quantity of work necessary for success!

Employees at all levels have a desire to satisfy the boss. However, human nature being what it is, some will try to get by with doing a little less than others.

All employees want to know what is expected of them, and good leaders make it very clear as to what they want.

They also firmly make it clear that their reasonable standards are the minimum standards expected, and that less will not be tolerated.

People want responsibility and will accept a challenge to perform at higher than minimum levels, *if* they are treated right.

Be sure that your standards are set at reasonable and attainable levels.

> *Always do more than is required of you.*
> General George S. Patton

GETTING PEOPLE INVOLVED

It is not just a job, it is *their* job.

Ask their opinions, get their perspectives, listen to their ideas and let them be innovative.

People want interesting jobs and new challenges. Help them get excited and get involved!

They'll be happier and so will you.

> *An automobile goes nowhere efficiently unless it has a quick, hot spark to ignite things, to set the cogs of the machine in motion. So I try to make every player on my team feel he's the spark keeping our machine in motion.*
>
> Knute Rockne

NOT CODDLING POOR PERFORMERS

Occasionally, despite their best leadership skills, leaders will find someone who just won't perform up to standards. They violate basic rules and won't perform as they are expected to.

Try to get that employee involved, using everything you can think of, but don't carry them on your back forever.

Some people would say it's only one person, and that they aren't *that* far below standards.

True leaders either get them to obey the rules and perform up to standards, or make other arrangements for them.

Other arrangements can include, transfer, reassignment, disciplinary action or dismissal.

One poor performer, if allowed to continue in the poor performance mode, can destroy morale and undermine an entire operation.

> *There is no use whatever trying to help people who do not help themselves. You cannot push anyone up a ladder unless he is willing to climb himself.*
>
> Andrew Carnegie

MANAGING CONFLICT

At times, reasonable people will disagree.

Conflict *within* a department can tear it apart. Leaders must step in and resolve the conflict before it has a chance to adversely affect the whole unit.

Conflict developing *between* departments is handled the same way—with your equal in the other department.

The important thing here is to be willing and able to handle conflict in an effective and timely fashion.

Naturally, the conflict must always be handled with a fair and equitable solution for all concerned. Leaving both sides as winners when the conflict ends is the work of a *true* leader.

> *There never was a time, in my opinion, some way could not be found to prevent the drawing of the sword.*
>
> General Ulysses S. Grant

CARING ABOUT EMPLOYEES

True leaders care about the employees they lead.

Employees are people, not machines.

Leaders know and understand their people. They treat them with dignity and respect. They protect them from abuses and help them with problems. They are understanding and accessible to them.

Leaders have respect for their employees and their abilities.

People want to work in a safe and healthy environment. It is up to the leaders to make sure that they do. Even if they have to protect employees from themselves at times by enforcing safety rules.

The employer generally gets the employees he deserves.
Sir Walter Gilbey

LOOSELY SUPERVISING SUBORDINATES

Leaders ensure that the work is being done, but allows employees the freedom to do their work in their own way. They encourage employees to make their own decisions and then support those decisions!

They don't stand over employees constantly, checking their every move. People want the freedom to do their work, *their* way.

Besides, leaders, if they are operating correctly as *true* leaders, should not have time to oversupervise. Leaders should have too much else to do.

> *Trust men and they will be true to you; treat them greatly and they will show themselves great.*
>
> Ralph Waldo Emerson

BUILDING A TEAM

Each individual must be treated like part of the team. They must each contribute to the team effort by doing what they do best for the benefit of themselves and the unit.

Leaders put round pegs in round holes, and square pegs in square holes.

In this way, those "pegs" are proud of their contribution; they are proud to be a part of the team, and they feel important.

Leaders should think and speak in terms of "We" and "Ours," and they should encourage their subordinates to do the same.

The man who gets the most satisfactory results is not always the man with the most brilliant single mind, but rather the man who can best coordinate the brains and talents of his associates.

W. Alton Jones

RESPECTING SUBORDINATES

Leaders find time to listen to their subordinates.

The ability to be creative, to have vision, and to be an informed professional is not limited to management personnel alone. Subordinates often have valuable ideas for improving products and services.

True leaders treat each person as a unique individual. They recognize their strengths and weaknesses, and accept both.

> *Men are respectable only as they respect.*
> Ralph Waldo Emerson

ENCOURAGING SUBORDINATES

People want to learn and grow. They also want the opportunity to advance.

Leaders show employees where they can go in the organization and help them to get there.

They give of themselves, their time, their knowledge, their experience; to ensure that their subordinates can grow. They arrange for employees to have opportunities for training and advancement.

They don't worry about people leaving their unit because they have their employees' long-term welfare in mind.

What better position could they be in than to get promoted and find several of their former employees in that new unit—employees that they encouraged and assisted to be all that they could be? The result of a leader's past support will be loyalty that cannot be obtained any other way.

> *It is . . . management's job to enable the enterprise and each of its members to grow and develop.*
> Peter F. Drucker

TEACHING EFFECTIVELY

Perhaps no other area of leadership can have such long-lasting and rewarding results.

We can all remember those whom we worked under who took us under their wings and "showed us the ropes."

As a leader, it is you who are now obligated to do the same for your subordinates.

When the people you teach reach higher positions in the organization, you will feel the rewards of a teacher.

In the interim, your teaching efforts will make your employees better workers, which will benefit you, your unit, and the organization.

> *A teacher affects eternity; no one can tell where his influence stops.*
>
> Henry Adams

BEING ACCESSIBLE

This doesn't mean just physically accessible.

This means that employees must feel comfortable about coming to you to ask questions, get advice and occasionally just to get your opinions on their future.

You should be out among your subordinates often. Out where *they* work! Out there to get their perspectives, to explain company policies and goals, and to get to know them as people.

They will learn to feel comfortable with you, and will feel free to discuss issues, ideas and problems with you. That open communication will benefit you, your employees and the organization.

It takes a great man to make a good listener.
Sir Arthur Helps

*L*EADERS RECOGNIZE that only a limited number of goals can be pursued at any one time.

They must accurately determine what is important, and what is less important.

The most important priorities receive the first attention. Then everything else follows in descending order of importance.

Meeting a deadline on a trivial matter is good, but not when a major project is put hopelessly behind as a result.

Leaders must use their judgment, after gathering all the facts and analyzing them, to be sure all of their priorities are in the right place.

> *It is best to do things systematically, since we are only humans, and disorder is our worst enemy.*
>
> Hesiod

THINKING MULTIFACETEDLY

Leaders are able to handle a variety of projects at one time.

Their thoughts are organized into a series of channels. They are able to select the correct channel, tune their mind to it, immediately evaluate the status of it, and then receive or give information about it.

The next phone call or other input is about another project. Again they switch to the appropriate channel and effectively handle the situation.

The person who can only think in singular terms will have great difficulty in being a *true* leader.

> *I do not feel obliged to believe that that same God who has endowed us with sense, reason, and intellect has intended us to forego their use.*
>
> Galileo Galilei

USING GOOD JUDGMENT

Basic judgment skills should be honed by education, training and years of diversified experience.

All of these factors will combine to allow the leader to gather the facts, analyze them, project solutions, evaluate them and arrive at a decision that is fair and sound for all concerned.

> *Reason and judgment are the qualities of a leader.*
> Tacitus

MAKING DECISIONS

To be considered a leader without having the fortitude to make sound decisions in a timely fashion is unthinkable.

There is no place for the faint of heart when it comes to decision-making. Decision avoidance is unacceptable.

Some decisions are better than others, but leaders make very few *wrong* decisions. Leaders do their best and move on to bigger and better things.

In addition, leaders will, at times, have to make unpopular decisions.

They may also have to implement unpopular decisions made above their level. However, *true* leaders can do it in such a way that subordinates understand, just as leaders understand, that the decision has been made and must be carried out.

> *The difference between a successful person and others is not a lack of strength, not a lack of knowledge, but rather a lack of will.*
>
> Vince Lombardi

DIAGNOSING WELL

Leaders can analyze the facts quickly to prevent or solve a problem.

Their research, knowledge and experience allows them to know a system so well that dealing with it is often second nature.

Like well-trained mechanics, they can identify a problem and correct it before it gets worse.

> *Life is short, art long, opportunity fleeting, experience treacherous, judgment difficult.*
>
> Hippocrates

HANDLING FRUSTRATION WELL

On a daily basis, leaders will deal with numerous people, many of who will make conflicting demands on them, their people and their resources.

Incompetent managers will become frustrated and seriously stressed. However, competent leaders will sort things out, set priorities and get done what they can.

Leaders must also develop the ability to accept those things that they do not have the power or the ability to change.

> *I sit here all day trying to persuade people to do the things they ought to have sense enough to do without my persuading them.*
>
> Harry S. Truman

HANDLING STRESS WELL

The best leaders become cooler when the heat is turned up.

Stress merely arouses their competitive spirit, allowing them to think more clearly and quickly, and to act with decisiveness.

Crisis is the true test of a person's leadership ability.

> *The ultimate measure of a man is not where he stands in moments of comfort and convenience, but where he stands at times of challenge and controversy.*
>
> Martin Luther King, Jr.

ALWAYS HAVING A SENSE OF DIRECTION

Leaders know where they are going. They also have a plan to get there.

When they are out in front, leading the way, their subordinates will follow them, and they will get there too.

> *If you don't know where you want to go, it doesn't matter how you get there.*
>
> Lewis Carroll

SIMPLIFYING COMPLEX SITUATIONS

Leaders make sense out of what appears to be too complex, and enjoy working in such a complex environment.

However, they always keep the original goal in mind.

They don't get caught up in all the ancillary problems and details.

Keeping their thoughts—and their subordinates' actions—constantly headed in the right direction is the mark of a *true* leader.

> *Everything should be made as simple as possible, but not simpler.*
>
> Albert Einstein

LOOKING AHEAD

True leaders are always looking ahead, projecting results and evaluating their current position.

They are always checking to be sure that they and their subordinates can adjust to future contingencies.

Their foresight forestalls and foretells future problems.

> *He is most free from danger, who, even when safe, is on his guard.*
>
> Publilius Syrus

EXPEDITING

Leaders keep the work from getting bogged down.

When a lack of supplies threatens to slow production, they expedite the arrival of the needed supplies.

When bureaucratic red tape threatens to adversely affect their people or their unit, they cut through the red tape to keep things moving.

Leaders ensure that everybody has what they need to get the job done, when they need it, whether it is supplies, people, cooperation or guidance.

We can lick gravity, but sometimes the paperwork is overwhelming.

Wernher von Braun

KEEPING LIFE IN BALANCE

"All work and no play makes Jack a dull boy."

In order to be considered a *successful* person, you must be successful in a variety of areas. Some of the more important, and often conflicting, areas are job, family, public service, church, social life, and recreation.

Focusing too much of your energy in one place will make you like Jack: dull and boring.

Balance all facets of your life to enjoy it to the fullest.

No pleasure endures, unseasoned by variety.
Publilius Syrus

RUNNING EFFECTIVE MEETINGS

Too many otherwise productive hours are spent in long, boring, marginally productive meetings.

Leaders look at the alternatives:

Don't conduct a meeting if a memo will do.

Don't send a memo if a phone call will do.

If there is information to disseminate, maybe you should convey it face to face. Out where the action is! Among your people.

However, if you must have meetings, they should always:

Start on time.

Have a definite agenda.

End as quickly as possible.

Get everyone back to what they do best! WORKING!

> *The length of a meeting rises with the square of the number of people present.*
>
> Eileen Shanahan

ASKING FOR INPUT

Leaders always ask for input from:
    Subordinates.
    Peers.
    Superiors.
    And from outside sources.
    True leaders' egos aren't fragile. Leaders recognize that no single person can have all of the answers all of the time, and that they can always learn from others.

> *There are no problems we cannot solve together, and very few that we can solve by ourselves.*
>   Lyndon Baines Johnson

COMMUNICATING *VERY* WELL

Leaders are articulate.

Their communications, both written and verbal, are clear and concise. They are easily understood.

Leaders follow up verbal communications with written communications, so that there are no mis-understandings.

Leaders speak and write in terms of the education, maturity level and experience of the recipient.

> *Communication is something so simple and difficult that we can never put it in simple words.*
>
> T. S. Matthews

CHAPTER FIVE: A LEADER UNDERSTANDS

*E*MPLOYEES AND MANAGERS follow guidelines and rules. They know what should be done, and they do it, but often without the full understanding of why they are following the rules or doing the work they are assigned.

Leaders, on the other hand, understand all of the components of the system, how they interact, and how success by each component results in the overall success of a project.

This total understanding should be your goal if you wish to be a *true* leader.

> *There is a great difference between knowing and understanding: you can know a lot about something and not really understand it.*
>
> Charles F. Kettering

THE LEADERSHIP ROLE

Leaders understand their role as leaders. They understand that they are needed. Without good leaders, little of consequence could be accomplished.

Successful leaders enjoy their leadership role.

They find it satisfying to watch people learn, grow and succeed under their leadership.

True leaders understand that leadership is an attitude and that the more their employees succeed, the more enjoyable it is to be a leader.

> *It's not work if you love what you are doing.*
> Malcolm Forbes

THE ORGANIZATION

Leaders understand:

The structure of it.

The purpose of it.

Its role and position in the industry.

The leader understands who does what, and why they do it.

Most of all, leaders understand where they fit into the organizational structure.

> *If everybody contemplates the infinite, instead of fixing the drains, many of us will die of cholera.*
>
> John Rich

THE BOSS

Everyone has a boss, even a leader.

Understanding that the boss wants to get the job done, with as few problems as possible, can help guide a leader to take the necessary actions to get the job done right.

Of course, a leader also understands that the boss needs to be kept informed, and *never* wants to be embarrassed.

> *Before you have an argument with your boss, you'd better take a good look at both sides—his side and the outside.*
>
> Unknown

THE EMPLOYEES

Leaders study their employees' needs and desires.

Here is the "Short Course" in understanding what employees *really* work for:

1. Appreciation of the work they do.
2. Being a part of something—belonging.
3. Being respected and understood.
4. Job security.
5. Good wages.
6. Interesting work.
7. Personal growth and/or promotions.
8. Good working conditions.
9. Emotional security and stability.
10. A sense of personal power.

Stop and think about these 10 items. Aren't they the same things that you want?

> *Leadership is the art of getting somebody else to do something you want done; because he wants to do it.*
> Dwight D. Eisenhower

THE GOALS

Organizational goals come in at least three sizes:
Short-term, intermediate, and long-term.

Understanding the goals of the organization, of your unit and of the people surrounding you will help you reach those goals.

Leaders also understand their own goals and how to reach them. All of your decisions must be made with those goals in mind.

You must never lose sight of your personal and organizational goals. You must relentlessly pursue them at all times.

The person who makes a success of living is the one who seeks his goal steadily and aims for it unswervingly.
Cecil B. DeMille

THE RULES

Knowing the rules is not enough. Anyone who can memorize the Pledge of Allegiance can learn a set of rules.

The important thing is to know why the rules exist and how they came to be there.

Every organization has a different set of rules. That alone should tell you something. Look at the rules of your organization in light of its history and culture of your organization.

What is the goal of a particular rule? What are the consequences to the unit if it is broken?

Asking these questions and examining the answers will help you develop an understanding of why the rules are the rules, and the importance of following them for both you and your employees.

The man who commands efficiently must have obeyed others in the past, and the man who obeys dutifully is worthy of being some day, a commander.

Cicero

POWER

The concept of power is interesting. It can be used and abused.

A leader understands its sources—how to get them and how to keep them.

Don't confuse force with power:

A million troops in a war is force; however,

a woman winking at a man is power.

A capable leader understands this total concept of power.

He or she understands what makes the powerful, powerful. A leader also understands that the perception of power is often as great as, or greater than, having the actual power itself.

A *true* leader is also very careful to use power sparingly, if at all.

Be sensitive to where power exists in your organization if you wish to be a successful leader.

> *Nearly all men can stand adversity, but if you want to test a man's character, give him power.*
>
> Abraham Lincoln

POLITICS

Politics: who is saying what, to whom, and why?

You don't have to *play* politics, as long as you acknowledge the existence of the political structure and understand that politics have a substantial, and sometimes subtle, influence on nearly every phase of human interaction.

A leader must be cognizant of the internal and external politics involved in running any type of organization. Failure to understand these politics has been the downfall of many otherwise very capable individuals.

Fact: the higher one goes in an organization, the more politically astute one must become in order to survive.

> *Knowledge of human nature is the beginning, and the end, of political education.*
>
> Henry Adams

DISCIPLINE

Leaders understand the concepts of both positive and negative discipline!

They understand the necessity of discipline, and the reasons for maintaining it.

One can always tell an individual who understands discipline because he/she is disciplined.

Employees want fair and reasonable discipline in the workplace and a leader who can use discipline sparingly.

Speak softly, and carry a big stick—you will go far.
Theodore Roosevelt

TIMING

If showing up is 90 percent of life, then showing up at the right time is the other 10 percent.

Leaders with a good sense of timing know:

When to speak.

When to shut up.

When to push a point.

When to back off.

True leaders know when to express an opinion and when to wait until they are asked.

> *To everything there is a season, and a time to every purpose under heaven.*
>
> Ecclesiastes 3:1

MORALE

Good morale is critical to the well-being of any work unit.

Morale is primarily a local issue. Yes, policies of the administration and other outside influences can have some effect on it, but the leader of the individual unit, by far, has the greatest influence on the morale of subordinates.

A leader's day-to-day actions and attitudes are critical. When a leader is fair, professional and optimistic, morale in the unit will be good. Good morale leads to success, and success leads to better morale.

> *When dealing with people, remember you are not dealing with creatures of logic, but with creatures of emotions, creatures bristled with prejudice and motivated by pride and vanity.*
>
> Dale Carnegie

LIMITATIONS

Leaders understand their own limitations, but they are not necessarily limited by them.

As an example, budgets can limit available resources, but a *true* leader will find a way to get the job done with the resources available. Staffing three shifts can't be done with only two people, but a *true* leader will make the most efficient use of those two people to cover the shifts.

Time is always a limitation. Rome wasn't built in a day. Yet, a *true* leader will make the most efficient use of the time available. Luckily, there are some things that know no limits:

Dreams.

Human ingenuity.

Love.

Even though you may not be able to conquer the whole world, you can comfortably conquer a small part of it, even taking into account many of your limitations.

Problems are only opportunities in work clothes.
Henry J. Kaiser

MISTAKES

In an imperfect world, mistakes and their ensuing problems are inevitable.

Often, it's a matter of when, not if, mistakes will occur.

When mistakes occur, leaders become experts in damage control, getting things back on track as soon as possible and minimizing the effect of the error.

Leaders must always be willing to underwrite the honest errors of their subordinates.

True leaders tolerate, and sometimes even encourage, honest mistakes. Why? Because innovation and imagination should have no set boundaries. Some of the greatest discoveries of all time were "mistakes."

> *Results! Why, man, I have gotten a lot of results. I know several thousand things that won't work.*
>
> Thomas A. Edison

EMPATHY

Empathy is the ability to understand another person's situation.

Stop and think about someone else's goals, motivations, feelings and concerns.

Once you understand your subordinates' position and why they are in it, you will be in a much better position to lead them in the proper direction.

> *A man always has two reasons for doing anything—a good reason and the real reason.*
>
> J. P. Morgan

HUMOR

In times of crisis, leaders must reduce a problem to real-world standards. They see the comedy of the situation and clear the stress and tension from the air through their own sense of humor.

Subordinates need this type of release in order to relax, reevaluate, and reprioritize their goals. Then they can refocus on what *really* needs to be done to correct the problems and get the job done.

The simple "humor relief" created by a leader can be the difference between success and failure. A *true* leader understands that.

> *Humor is an affirmative of dignity; a declaration of man's superiority to all that befalls him.*
>
> Romain Gary

THE FUTURE

The future represents what is new. It represents change and innovation. It represents hope and the results of past efforts and attitudes.

The present is important, and we must learn from the past. But the future provides a vision not yet attained—a target to aim for.

A leader understands the importance of that vision for success.

> *I like the dreams of the future, better than the history of the past.*
>
> Thomas Jefferson

❧ CHAPTER SIX: A LEADER LEADS BY

$\mathcal{A}$T THIS POINT, you should be gaining an understanding that becoming a leader is an incremental process.

Becoming an effective *supervisor* requires certain skills, which we have already reviewed.

Becoming an effective *manager* requires another set of skills.

Logically, then, one would think that becoming an effective leader requires yet another set of skills.

Here, we present the leadership skills which build on all of the skills previously covered. It's a formula for your success.

Happiness lies in the joy of achievement and the thrill of creative effort.

Franklin D. Roosevelt

ASSUMING THE LEADERSHIP ROLE

To be appointed to a leadership position is not sufficient to make you a leader.

You must, after being appointed, take charge and begin leading.

Too many people feel that they have *arrived* when they get promoted. The wise know that promotion is just the beginning.

A leader who assumes the leadership role is much more effective than those who try to succeed by mere position.

It is easier to assume your role once you understand that people want and need to be led by a competent leader. You are there to help them, as well as yourself, by giving them direction.

When in charge, take charge!
Unknown

THINKING IN TERMS OF SOLUTIONS

One seldom has to look for problems. They have a natural way of making themselves known.

One does, however, have to look for solutions to those problems.

Rather than expend energy worrying and placing blame, leaders just solve the problem.

Then they go one step further and take action to ensure that a similar problem doesn't occur in the future.

> *The block of granite which is an obstacle in the pathway of the weak, becomes a stepping-stone in the pathway of the strong.*
>
> Thomas Carlyle

SURROUNDING THEMSELVES
WITH COMPETENCE

Leaders are not afraid of subordinates taking their jobs.

Quite the contrary: leaders recruit the best subordinates they can find. Then, they train them thoroughly so they can not only do their job, but so they can also fill in for the leader when necessary.

This ensures that the leader gets maximum performance, will be able to take time off, and can be promoted to a higher job, because they have arranged a suitable replacement for their current job.

Quality subordinates are a result of, and a course of, strong leadership.

There is something that is much more scarce, something rarer than ability. It is the ability to recognize ability.
Robert Half

HANDLING AMBIGUITY WELL

Life is so simple at the bottom. The boss gives you a specific job to do and you do it.

As you move up the hierarchy, the work becomes less defined. The boss gives you a mandate to solve a problem, and gives you little else. It is up to you to define the parameters of the task, figure out how to finance it, and find the time to get it done.

Leaders thrive on this kind of work. Ambiguity is a type of freedom for them to be creative and innovative. It challenges them and allows them to turn their own thoughts into actions.

The initial lack of direction would bother many employees, but not a *true* leader.

> *I believe that the true road to preeminent success in any*
> *line, is to make yourself master of that line.*
>
> Andrew Carnegie

EXHIBITING GOOD COMMON SENSE

Is common sense inborn? Maybe.

The result of experience? Maybe.

The combination of intelligence, knowledge and experience?

Probably!

The experts can argue what constitutes *common sense* until the end of time.

However, the fact remains that a *true* leader has it.

Period!

> *Common sense is the knack of seeing things as they are, and doing things as they ought to be done.*
>
> Josh Billings

TAKING RISKS

Leaders take *calculated* risks!

Leaders are not foolhardy, wild-eyed maniacs who throw away the rule-book.

On the contrary: leaders continually evaluate the elements of a risky project in comparison to the potential for gain from taking those risks.

They speak out in the heat of controversy. They take a stand when right, but not necessarily popular. They dare to try new ideas, sure in their own minds that their ideas will work.

They do not risk the safety of their subordinates or someone else's career—only their own.

If nothing is ever ventured, then nothing is ever gained.

> *It is impossible to win the great prizes of life without running risks.*
>
> Theodore Roosevelt

STRIVING TO BE THE BEST

In everything they do.

Leaders also instill this attribute in their subordinates.

Leaders seek to be the best—for their own satisfaction.

> *Get a good idea and stay with it. Dog it, and work at it until it's done and done right.*
>
> Walt Disney

TAKING RESPONSIBILITY

True leaders are in charge, and they are responsible for every facet of the project.

When it is successful, they are the ones responsible. When it is unsuccessful, they are also responsible.

Taking responsibility relieves others, and shows them who the *true* leader really is.

> *A chief is a man who assumes responsibility. He says, "I was beaten." He does not say, "My men were beaten." Thus speaks a real man.*
>
> Antoine de Saint-Exupery

TURNING ADVERSITY INTO OPPORTUNITY

When handed a lemon, make lemonade.

The leader follows this advice and looks for any opportunity to combat, and thrive against, adversity.

Every cloud has a silver lining. *True* leaders look for that silver lining at every opportunity of adversity.

> *Since the house is on fire, let us warm ourselves.*
>
> Italian Proverb

RUNNING AHEAD OF THE PACK

Leaders are a little more progressive.
  A little more innovative.
  A little more creative.
  They take that extra step.
  Spend a little more effort.
  Get a little more accomplished.
  Get a few more results.
  They get promoted a little sooner.
  However, they can't run too far ahead of the pack.
They need support from others to be successful. If
they're too far ahead, others can't keep up. If oth-
ers can't keep up, they can't help their leaders if
they encounter trouble.
  So, unless you want to go it completely alone, keep
ahead, but not too far ahead.

> *It is a mistake to look too far ahead. Only one link in the*
> *chain of destiny can be handled at a time.*
> Winston Churchill

ALWAYS GOING FORWARD

Leaders are always going forward. Sometimes in tiny steps, but usually in quantum leaps.

A leader's group is the first to be computerized, first to try new technologies, and first in efficiency and productivity.

They don't increase their productivity by hundredths of a percent, they increase it by full percentage points. They can even double or triple past performances.

True leaders make things happen in a big way.

> *Even if you're on the right track, you'll get run over if you just sit there.*
>
> Arthur Godfrey

EXAMPLE

One Fortune 500 executive told his people, "You may do anything you see me doing."

Subordinates will emulate, consciously or subconsciously, their bosses.

If you are forward-thinking, innovative, and progressive, then your department will move consistently forward.

True leaders are also willing to roll up their shirt sleeves and do whatever is necessary to make a project succeed. Their commitment and dedication in such a situation sets the example for all of their people.

True leaders are excellent role models.

> *The example of good men is visible philosophy.*
> English Proverb

HAVING VISION

To be able to visualize the completed project, the final goal and all of its rewards and consequences, is the ultimate test for *true* leaders.

In addition to visualizing "the dream," they must also be able to visualize each task that must be completed, and the integration of those tasks to successfully complete the project.

Such vision is dependent upon all of the attributes, actions and efforts described in previous sections of this book.

To *true* leaders, vision defines the final goal, and action is the path that leads to the vision.

*We have always held to the hope, the belief, the conviction
that there is a better life, a better world, beyond the horizon.*
Franklin D. Roosevelt

CHAPTER SEVEN: A LEADER AVOIDS

*T*HERE ARE CERTAIN things in the real world that can cancel out all of your preparations and good intentions for becoming a *true* leader.

Here we present a host of them. Avoid them if you want to be successful.

> *This is a hard and precarious world where every mistake*
> *and infirmity must be paid for in full.*
>
> Clarence Day

BEING LATE

For anything!

If you show up late for a meeting, you are wasting not only your time, but that of others as well.

In any industry, time is money.

If you are late in the morning, take extended breaks or two hour lunches, your employees will follow your example.

> *Dost thou love life? Then do not squander time, for that is the stuff life is made of.*
>
> Benjamin Franklin

OVERSPECIALIZATION

In general, leaders have a wide variety of knowledge on many subjects. Even though they may also have a specialty area, they avoid overspecialization.

Overspecialization in one area tends to make a person a technician, rather than a leader.

> *The world's great men have not commonly been great scholars, nor its great scholars great men.*
> Oliver Wendell Holmes

BLAMING OTHERS

When in a position of leadership, everything that occurs is your responsibility, even the errors.

Rather than spending effort in placing the blame on others, your job is to minimize the damage, and to take the steps necessary so that the problem does not recur in the future.

The buck stops here!
Harry S. Truman

CRITICISM OF OTHERS

Leaders find the strong points of individuals and focus on those.

Openly criticizing *subordinates* is a counterproductive activity since they will not want to perform for a critic.

Openly criticizing *superiors* is a sure way to shorten your career in that organization.

> *He that is without sin among us, let him cast the first stone.*
>
> John 8:7

JEALOUSY

Leaders focus on their own career and accomplishments.

Others, including those in competition with you, will also garner accomplishments and awards.

Rather than wasting energy on jealousy, share their joy of accomplishment.

Seek them out as friends and colleagues. Learn from them.

Winners associate with winners!

> *Of all the passions, jealousy is that which exerts the hardest service and pays the bitterest wages.*
> Charles Cabet Colton

EXCESSIVE PRESSURE

Leaders prevent excessive pressure on both the receiving and giving ends.

Set realistic goals for yourself and your subordinates.

If an unrealistic task is given to you, realize it and present the facts to your boss to show that their expectations should be modified.

Excessive pressure on employees serves no purpose and often kills initiative and creativity at all levels.

> *We are more often frightened than hurt; our troubles spring more often from fancy than reality.*
>
> Seneca

UNION CONFLICTS

Preparation and fundamental fairness are your best allies to avoid problems in this area.

Read and understand the union contracts of everyone in your work unit. Then, follow them to the letter.

Unions developed in response to management abuses. If you treat everyone as you would like to be treated, you will avoid conflicts with union representatives.

> *It is one of the characteristics of a free and democratic modern nation that it have free and independent labor unions.*
>
> Franklin D. Roosevelt

SECOND-GUESSING

Also known as "Monday-morning quarterbacking."
    Subordinates should be encouraged to make their own decisions. It is then incumbent upon the leader to support those decisions whenever possible.

> *What a man dislikes in his superiors, let him not display in the treatment of his inferiors.*
>
> Tsang Sin

ARROGANCE

Don't be caught up in the power and prestige of your position. Nothing is beneath a *true* leader.

You must always be willing to help subordinates, even in the most mundane tasks.

Remember that you will occasionally make errors. You know that, and your employees know that.

If you have an arrogant attitude, you can expect no help from your subordinates in preventing or correcting your errors.

> *To be vain of one's rank or place, is to show that one is below it.*
>
> Stanislas I

WASTE

A major part of your job is to effectively utilize human and other resources to get the job done.

Wasting any of your resources decreases the efficiency of your unit, and is a poor business practice in any industry.

Take the time to plan effectively and ensure that waste is cut to a bare minimum.

> *Waste neither time nor money, but make the best use of both.*
>
> Benjamin Franklin

CONFLICTS OF INTEREST

Keep in mind that the *perception* of a conflict of interest can be nearly as bad as the real thing.

Avoid kickbacks, special favors, and preferential treatment in your dealings with suppliers and associates. Don't give them, or receive them.

Just as honesty begets honesty, corruption begets corruption.

> *There is no odor so bad as that which arises from goodness tainted.*
>
> Henry David Thoreau

LYING

At all cost!
   Never lie to your people or anyone else!

> *When a person cannot deceive himself, the chances are against his being able to deceive other people.*
> Mark Twain

UNSAVORY CHARACTERS

Who are your friends and associates?

Are they the kind of people you should be associating with?

Are they "Leadership Material?"

> *Associate with men of good quality if you esteem your own reputation; for it is better to be alone than in bad company.*
>
> George Washington

GAMBLING

Whether it's the office sports pool, or phone calls to your "bookie," gambling gives the perception of impropriety and a lack of discipline on your part.

True leaders avoid it because they know it is a "loser's" game.

> *The best throw of the dice is to throw them away.*
> English Proverb

SEXUAL HARASSMENT

In order to avoid sexual harassment, a leader must know and understand what constitutes sexual harassment in the workplace.

Part of your responsibility as a leader is to prevent your subordinates from perpetrating, or being a victim of, sexual harassment.

Ignoring the reality of sexual harassment in the workplace will clearly jeopardize your otherwise successful career.

> *Injustice anywhere is a threat to justice everywhere.*
> Martin Luther King, Jr.

FINANCIAL PROBLEMS

If you can't control your own personal finances, how can you expect an employer to trust you to handle their resources effectively?

The same rules that apply to business can also apply to the management of your personal life.

Planning, coordinating, effective utilization of resources and vision are just a few of the traits that should apply to your personal life as well as your business life.

> *He that has a penny in his purse, is worth a penny:*
> *Have and you shall be esteemed.*
>
> Petronius

SICK LEAVE

When you are sick, take sick leave.

If you are healthy, go to work.

Rest assured that the one day you call in on sick leave to go to the ball game, will be the one time you make the 11 o'clock news as a sports highlight, catching a home-run ball.

If you abuse your benefits, your subordinates will also abuse theirs, and you will often be short-handed and short on respect.

> *I would give no thought of what the world might say of me, if I could only transmit to posterity the reputation of an honest man.*
>
> Sam Houston

GOSSIP AND RUMORS

Avoid gossip; control rumors!

> *Silence is the ultimate weapon of power.*
> Charles de Gaulle

BLIND LOYALTY

Loyalty is a leadership trait, but blind loyalty is dangerous.

True loyalty to all involves dedication, support, and sometimes disagreement in an effort to prevent future problems.

However, you cannot support superiors or subordinates who engage in illegal or immoral activities regardless of their motivation.

Avoiding *blind* loyalty serves the interests of everyone.

> *If the blind lead the blind, both shall fall into the ditch.*
> Matthew 15:14

ALCOHOL AND DRUGS

Having too many drinks at the company party has brought down more careers than any other single factor.

Individuals with so little self-control that they fall prey to excessive drinking, or drug abuse, cannot be expected to have enough self-control to run a department or organization.

Drunkenness is the failure of a man to control his thoughts.

David Graysin

BURNOUT

The business world is tough! But for a good leader, the difficulties are a challenge.

Nevertheless, burnout can occur in any occupation—in two years or 20 years.

To prevent burnout, keep meeting new challenges, either within your organization or in other organizations.

When the work you once found challenging and even fun has turned into drudgery and a bore, it is time to move on.

A burned-out leader is no leader at all.

All looks yellow to a jaundiced eye.
Alexander Pope

ILLEGAL ACTS

Avoid illegal acts on the job and off the job!

Say no to bribes, kickbacks, and special gifts.

Say no to discrimination, labor law violations, and safety and health code violations.

You must know the law and the consequences of your actions in these areas, or risk seriously damaging your career.

A law is valuable not because it is the law, but because there is right in it.

Henry Ward Beecher

EMOTIONAL TRAPS

Employees may try to "dump" personal problems on you.

Go ahead and try to help them, but don't get directly or emotionally involved in their problems or lives.

Remember, as a professional you can listen, recommend and assist, but you cannot live their lives for them.

Avoid the emotional traps they may set for you.

> *The intellect is always fooled by the heart.*
> François de La Rochefoucauld

LOSS OF TEMPER

There is little in the world worthy of losing your temper about.

Yet frustrations in the workplace are common and can be difficult to deal with.

As a leader, always try to stay in control. Discuss problems openly with the people involved. Be firm in your demands, but remain in control.

Superiors, suppliers, peers, customers, and sub-ordinates will sometimes be infuriating, but losing your temper will probably only compound the problem instead of solving it.

> *When angry, count ten before you speak. If very angry, a hundred.*
>
> Thomas Jefferson

*T*RUE LEADERS ARE a combination of understanding supervisors and competent managers. They have an understanding of the present, and a vision for the future.

To be successful as a leader in any industry, you must:

Prepare to be a leader.

Understand leadership.

And then be prepared to assume the leadership role in your organization.

Your journey must not end here. In fact, your journey will never end as a *true* leader.

Leadership is about reaching for the stars, and when you reach one, reach for the next one.

It's exciting, it's fun, and it's the essence of life.

The talent of success is nothing more than doing what you can do well, and doing well whatever you do.
Henry Wadsworth Longfellow

*T*WENTY-FIVE negative behavioral characteristics that can hinder potential leaders:

Lack of knowledge
Disinterest in work
Negative attitude
Constantly complaining personality
Lack of social skills
Self-centered demeanor
Inability to speak in public
Arrogance
Interruption of others
Poor appearance
Indecision
Failure to listen
Poor posture
Tendency to talk too much
Insecurity
Impatience
Irresponsibility
Lack of enthusiasm
Lack of dependability
Argumentativeness
Poor personal hygiene
Preoccupation
Lack of personal integrity
Overreaction
Lack of concern for others

*T*WENTY-FIVE positive behavioral characteristics that can help potential leaders:

Sociability
Trustworthiness
Warmth
Supportiveness
Independence
Dependability
Leadership incentive
Competitive nature
Assertiveness
Ability to listen
Fairness
Loyalty
Flexibility
Reliability
Generosity
Dynamic personality
Adaptability
Tough-mindedness
Versatility
Cooperation
Risk-taking
Approachability
Ability to cope
Orientation to people
Responsibility

About the Author

Roger Fulton has over 25 years of practical supervisory and leadership experience in both public and private sector organizations. He has studied the attributes of successful supervisors, managers, and leaders as an avocation, as well as for his own success. In addition to his first book, *Common Sense Supervision*, Mr. Fulton has published dozens of magazine and journal articles on the subject of management and supervision. Currently, he resides in Hayes, Virginia where he is the President of Knight Management Corporation, a management training and consulting firm he founded in 1986.